RE**CONSTRUCTIONS**

BRADLEY TRUMPFHELLER

SIBLING RIVALRY PRESS
DISTURB/ENRAPTURE
LITTLE ROCK, ARKANSAS

TABLE OF CONTENTS ::

[desire] marks the limit at which self-enclosure dissolves

and I dream a highway back to you

DO YOU KISS YOUR BOYFRIEND WITH THOSE VERBS

nothing worth saying stays still long enough to say it : moons moon & giggle
while whole flocks of I-statements cartwheel into whatever *city* signifies

this second, which it will never mean again, not even now. now is the word
we use to forgive ourselves for the future. instead of air, say airing.

how you looked after you piano-keyed my arching. & wouldn't
the stars starry that way. & wouldn't the science of it screech : taxing

& pyramidic : snap bracelet shuddering. & wasn't that the water of it.
you husked & yesterdayed. instead of loss, say every day we are moving

closer to when getting out of bed seems possible. instead of draw the curtains,
curtain up. drawn into fielding. never say heaven unless you mean the past

tense of to heave. as in I am heaven towards what, in our old tongues
bumbled with noise & stations of scam-crosses, we might have called

each other : which I now know only as the distance between the coin
lids your eyes decaded into & how you neolithic'd a grammar : bluet

esque : & how this rivering you unbecame beloved across

HEARING LOSS

after Ewan Hill

I assume a boys voice   is what unquiets the world

I matter   to the lips which matter back to me /

            the lions mane means the lions manly
    / the boys ring means the boys married

& in my mouth   in the parking lot   means i have been
               a bad bad bad girl

these satellites we misdiagnose as starlight   these
        cars passing   effortlessly / I assume every
sound I make   & cant distinguish
      was beautiful

           even the cardinal   I saw ruined
with windows was not   unlike the cardinal

/ its red instant of form
                  / & how as a child
      kneeling in leaves   I knew each animal
by voice / his legs

           tense against   my hands is
how I know   what Ive done

& tonight   I would like to leave him
               speechless / I write

      the dogwood   their goldish proof
    / my gown its drag   of vows

how again I   slip on his wedding
             ring &   wife / myself
    to its brief shard of noise

FROM RECONSTRUCTIONS

I won't explain. My aunts spell
                                        around the vanity mirror
& centerpiece me, my lips plummed,
                            my neck belled mid-flight.

        After the food's uncooked, the heirloom paring knife
stitched up the bell peppers & dark meat,
                                    after the fiddle leaves
            left their fiddles, the porch undressed of wasps & us
our old names—
                    right here. As if even the evening
            didn't let on. No parking lot, no gas stations. A scythe
of emptied prisons shudder
                                alongside the highway; bougainvillea
& gun oil in the sheets. All my cousins slow-dancing
            in their cowboy boots & antlers.

                    My mothers singing to the dogwood tree
        blooming black across my arm.

Your hand finally on the small of my back, without any kind of fear.

This time, I'll be a girl & you can be anything
alive. Take the rope off your wrists.
                            Somewhere far away from here,
        a star's unspooling its star-white curtain.

                    What happens if we begin already angels?

Press your ears to my wingspan. Hum a little.

We are the most possible kind of daughterhood.
                                    I promise.

Step into the light.
        Let me see the mark our rapture left behind.

EKPHRASIS, I GUESS

after Ewan Hill

Turning like any good daughter I spit
on the wedding picture I took from her
closet so they both seem to bend. Time is

so time. Let's say I put the sky to sleep
even if the stars are still in their sheds.
Okay. & someday, yeah. I do wanna

verb things like they looked good up there all
altar on their own, like I've swallowed too
many peach pits to not bolt any windows

this winter. Maybe I'm scared of heritage.
Or not. But I got these looks & locks
like I'm debutante. Where's my dance.

My model & make. It's true: I would make
a nightmare bridegroom. All disco lipgloss
& soft how I'm undoing. Call that our kind

of work. I got taught to tongue fruit
I found bleeding in the sheets. Like any good
headstone they bow so I'm catgut. They split

& I'm high-strung. They left, she's right, Dad's
half-seconds from stitching me into his collar
so I bite down past the peach fuzz, leave a mess

behind my neckline, plunge my ring fingers
in the stove pot like bloodthinner. Mom won't
say where she left what was left of her dress

so I put a third moon in the poem
to have enough dead light to dig by.

CATALOG OF DIVINE ENCOUNTERS
IN MOBILE COUNTY, AL

One man says he saw god at the pain clinic on Lafayette.
      Untucked shirt. Knife-white bandana, shadows boxing

under each drowned eye socket. There's never been a record

      of his hands, but that's never stopped me from painting
my nails. Some days we still find water jugs

      in the crawl space, already licked clean. Once I watched
         someone shoot a stray dog in the parking lot.

Across one page someone has only written   *Before the storm*

      How the neighbor boy felt pressed sweating against me.

Outside the liquor store, one of my cousins took a picture
    of a cross-shaped water stain.

                At last this lack of landscapes.

          The moon rises, then wheels, then steps
      into a bathtub, slick w/ its own shine.

Alligators laze in red mud, hunting their tails.
      Emptied lakes. A wake of widening eyes.

      On the bus back to the sticks, Uncle Buck met a girl
w/ a back-length braid who claimed she could heal the sick.

      A woman wrote that god shops at the Winn-Dixie
in cowboy boots & likes to click his spurs
         against the carts. Bullwhips of wind.
    Don't ask me about acrylics.

Between where he happens to my tongue & a window.

     Battlefielding. Bone up.
                Nobody heard my uncle

cadaver himself. Even birds no longer sound
        useful. When I pray for rain I pray

   the trees die before it comes.

ASPHYXIA

The day I realized I was already dying I dared myself to blood, took turns
tonguing ropeburn & threshold. As a boy, I'd watch my cousins stand
by the reservoir & drape their hands around each other's throats, see who
would buckle first, same spot the home guard hanged a man for desertion.

Of course every future's still stupid w/ bones. So tonight I'll be the best girl
dressed in lime juice & lingerie. My whole face a sundown, pink prom frock
left fetal on the tire pile. According to my uncle, the word *redneck* comes
from coal miners in West Virginia who wore blood-red handkerchiefs

around their collars when they shot cops for the right to unionize.
When I say this to the man making an exit of me at the club, he asks
why I care about people who want me dead. Still, how I'll buck
under his hand, spit scythed & sweat into pretense, my neck bled

to pass for paradise. I guess everyone knows utopia means no place,
the gates gilded & grafittied on graves. & I guess let's bless his dead,
decked in their expensive independence. Let's bless the boy who beat
a chest of rubies from my lips behind the gas station, bless the gas

its shawl of what's done in its name, bless the name, what muscle
it attends, bless the tongue, bless my tongue wrapped around another
boy's name while he chokes me into my ancestry: distant uncle trapped
in a collapsed shaft, cousin coughing up her stomach after her dealer

cut pills w/ rat poison, my face the color of my aunt's trailer's tarps
after the storms. One state, two state, red state, blue state, show me
the place no one wants me dead & I'll show you a girl dragging
a door from the water. Show me the man I can't make a song of

& I swear I won't resist.

FROM RECONSTRUCTIONS

But say we're not being hunted. Say instead
of shotguns, the men

hide rhinestones under their pillows.
Say the pillow I pressed

your face into had stolen every inch of cold

the city locked in necklaces of spit
& left stunned on the sidewalks.

Say spit like we could be caught.

Say city like we're nowhere
near going back.

Here are the mountains   flinching apart like doors

                His voice   clicking across the chalk-smear of silos

        Pistons   Lipstick   (my god)   Little dimples of wind

We're used to this

My god & the porchlights

                rattling off   one by one

MONUMENT

I take off that winter like a sports bra
eye bright woman with the roman nose, roman back-arch
denim on denim on I take off my skirt
in minutes and in front of no one
what kind of my people is this
a glass wren sweeping feathers from the musuem floor
how bone-rag, my time stutter
how three-windless, our nightjars & nightsticks
be serious

there was a boy, wolf's bane, bright
dress, fifth grade, what was
his name, worm
moon with her twenty-sided hands
and the milk-eyed curtain what room
falling where we I wonder
is he still a boy was he a boy then the mountain
snow melts the mountain flowers, seabirds sling
their diamonds, their syntax
my people, my exquisite corpse-breath
and pronoun and softly and sister
forgive me

I'm trying I'm trying I'm trying I'm trying
to write a history of us
without writing a history of us
being harmed

but when I think about that day
it is not your name I remember first

FROM RECONSTRUCTIONS

hills flatline in the rearview.

your hand rests into mine.   headlights
like an exile of clouds.

picture this:
                            downriver a man guns
his truck. everything smells like wings.

now one morning picture him & he's
wearing skirts like stunted light.   no, less.

crows shattered like crumbs across
our one good road.

speech fucks the air w/ a proof of us.

the gap between my teeth is the exact
width of a zipper.   trust me.

sheets   the thighs rubbed red   & roll
            & rain   obsessed itself down
the windows   & his yes   pinned up
against the   yes   crests &
    yes   the door we
                            forged it   shut

in the town my grandmothers are buried under
the collective noun for faggots is also a murder

I can remember so many nights

I can say they were like anything

as if any of us were uncounterfeit

my legs totaling
my legs   the body

at last a negative
of herself

EPITHALAMION

some birds in the longleaf & biking past daylight

doves whose I was terminal as spokes   as speaking
to a headstone   after living together
for thirty years my grandmothers are buried

in separate cemeteries   any altar
worth her weigh in marigold
gathers the body this way : gas station

coffee   birdhouses   the kudzu I could say curled
across their names   my mother's voice

on the phone reminding one of her
mothers her name   was not a country

the dandelions puckered & blown—   years ago
they piled in a car   drove east   hit water   kept driving

out to where she said she saw trees
shimmer in the break   the ocean was
a photograph of the ocean

brick whose I was opening the window
brick whose vow was the world
without glass & us

                        her dress   her bright blue suit jacket

forgive me   I'm trying to leave
a record of an impossible thing

                no wind chimes   no cemetery lawns

my mother's voice was not a country
until I drew the map   on my skin

doves whose I was ring-bearer   boy whose
I was flower girl

   & didn't the cabbage palms curtsy—
     & didn't the storm still wink—

I do know better than to want
weddings for us   but for once to see
my blood undressed of rust

how could I otherwise bear it?

TIME'S NOT AN ARROW, MORE THE PLACE AN ARROW TOUCHES US

Probably everywhere, there are rooms
full of people who do not love

each other yet. I arch
my back exactly like the steeple

we midwifed
from your breastbone—gold thread

on a white silk hoop; an egg
split down nothing like its middle.

Mostly I'm astonished we have an entire word
for the direction opposite a clock's

progress. Here's when I could say
something about my children, all the words

they will learn despite their new
sunless worlds & technologies—

but I won't have any children.
& if I did, what would they call me?

My first words were nonsense
shawled in sound

close enough to mother
for my mother

to know I saw her there.
Your first words are the kind of thing

you would have told me, small
effigy, while we waited

for the bus together,
or sat smoking on your back porch

while I congratulated the leaves
on their colors for the umpteenth

time this year. I'm losing
track of myself. I wanted

to begin this poem
w/ what I thought of first

the day we stopped speaking:
a bride in reverse; white road

flares being lit; woman
of me bowed

like a string into an antique light

Club bright, come blush & blurred. Bluish backdrops of noise
throbbing me into scene. His clink. Their collect & clamber. Ha.

An hour of men & no high beams. The city & the city
we slope to. We turn
          away from anything Pensacola in us.

& disco. & glitter on my skyline. Hips, clotted,
raw, unbuckled into boyhood.
       This ash-beckoning.   This cinder-signal.

& any chiasmus of hands make wanting seem ever. & I mean

that even my grandma's silver cross was a seam to tug

unartfully apart. Us, wet & weatherless things. Any unslanged

tongue. Vanity mirror in the bedsheets. One more one more hour.

Hill-at-night. Star-at-morning. What does the body,
in language, amount to? Wind. Wind, being wound.

These skyscrapers, zipped into lines. Choral & correct
as wings. My mother's hand pointing at the harbor
       makes it the harbor. Reckon the future were that:
         a port. A place to begin the work
of fastening. The body found
            & returned a name because sirens.
      Because red light. Her body & because
          she did not ever go missing. Red
light. Something like that.
          Curtains, unless. Unlessening. Ha.

The months have sisters here. The country
is stitched w/ a parataxis of gold.

Do not mistake me—
                there are worlds where all of this is true
        & we still do not survive.

Each tree a trace of us.

Stain, dark as a sheath   as a sheath.
Brightly.
                        No climate. No crownlands.

        Song is the catastrophe of speaking.

Everywhere we go has pronouns & we speak them, brightly.

Like a day. Like a day, shattering.

The hand & the hill-lights. The hand. The chapel. The Mountain Dew
wilting in his cupholder.

Cheap coffee, cigarettes. No egrets. Ha.

When I was alive, I told people I didn't believe in glass.

I loved a man who danced like a knife.
Ha. Like a knife.
                There are so many ways to be unfinished.

A year passes. A year
cedes.

PALINODE

again i make the boy again from dirt & daffodils : everybody

knows the story. saint whatever. all-country effigy. he stood

in front of me in a parking lot   with flowers in his hair.

my knees like knots in the mulch.   his zipper tasted

like a zipper.   years later i tell a room full of people i love

that he died drunk behind the wheel of a car : or he was hit

by the car : or he was the car   dim-eyed engine spun out

on the side of the road : or was it by the gas station on 11th

his veins dull & drawled with the same pills [   ] sold me

:   none of this is tender.

don't believe me.   there was never a boy until there was.

there was never a landscape   until it was stolen & written

into song. in a poem i will never publish i point at the grass

& everyone i love begins digging their own graves. & again

i am making this about me. the way a boy might take metal

in his mouth & blame everything after on shame.   or how

even the living when buried can be used   to hold up a flag.

29

SPECTACULAR, SPECTACULAR

In any kind of two-way glass daffodil there's the night
I put on my lover's dress & it fit me like a renaissance.

Snap the shoulder straps in time w/ the streetlights.
Click click goes the clock I disregard on principle. My,

what a wick you have. What an ankle-length shadow
I'm faking. My loud glade. My glued-shut bone gate.

Walk like this, go all the fairy lights. Put your hips
into me. Who gets undressed in this kind of story?

Click click. It's so heaven of us to think of anything
as untimely. My mom's thumb smearing the lipstick

off my collar, my mouth. I learned speech first
as distance, second as costume jewelry. I don't have

a lover. Any poem I wear anything gorgeous out of
is a lie. Who would remember me myself otherwise?

FROM RECONSTRUCTIONS

Across the sore blue particle board
       of the rest stop bathroom an hour out of Gulfport

someone scratched *There are trans people here—*

      the time it takes to travel
          from siren to fanfare. No moon

cycle, no rocket-eye. Some words
      water-towering up from a treeline, backlit

by neon. It won't matter
      how we're killed. Little glass bells

          undone w/ sounding. Any image begins

in violence. & our backs unclenched
      in the honeysuckle. & our faces

          in the bread aisle. *There are*
trans people   here. Here: my hands

          are an archive of their belly laugh.
     My breasts are the history of my breasts.

I lost I lost I lost something   in these hills.

         Little bells. Little bouquet
           of mirrors.

Say my name & I'll say yours back.
Say we belong here & I'll bewitch all the maps.

Blue lines for the rivers.
         Silver beds for the clouds.

Once, a boy pressed his right eye to his rifle's right.

O, the veil & the veil being lifted.

WHATEVER IS NOT PRAYER

I'm staying in tonight because the ceiling fan
looks like a can of Crisco you'd have cleaned

& kept the leftover grease in. There's the stories
we want to tell & then there's the stories

we should. I'm still not sure
which is better. Lately I've been letting

your cross polish my neckline
like sugar left on a welcome mat—

this doesn't mean
I forgive you. By now

it's become rehearsal:
the back of your hand,

how the climbing roses on the porch
smelled like the boy's navel, rain,

shore, shroud—how much do I need
to explain you to you? Every dream

I've had this month ends
in me pinning the photograph

of you holding hands
w/ the woman you loved

to my bedroom wall. Grandma,
this is where a better person would begin

to say something about grace.
The day I planted hyacinths

in your garden, the sound
of the truck engine idling

while you let the tape
finish. I don't remember

if you had a garden. Truth be told.
Truth, be told—be, hold me—

I'm so tired of elegies.

Where are you now
to tell me you did not survive

this long for me to touch a man
in public? Shame

is a translation of shame.
Before you died, I wonder

what world you imagined
I'd go on

to live in. To live
in. Grandma, I want you to see

you, alive
& humming

a lullaby into your lover's hair
while she makes you

both breakfast.
Unkie, tell me the moon

cares so much about us
that it has to stop

& start itself over again.
That kind of love.

TOMORROW, NO, TOMORROWER

From up here in the leaves' no-kidding goldishness
        you'd guess everyone was already in lovely w/ each
others' cheekbones. Infinity scarves
           & vanilla coffee, mint tea, warm whatever.
Cozy becoming the coming-at-the-seams, a couplet
        of verbs mid-bodily inexperience.
That man doing cartwheels is not wearing a shirt
& in any other life I'd want to be the double dare
           fanfaring a future so totally astonished
    by his nipples. This is what I mean

when I say things like *catastrophe*.
                Okay, fine. Just one more winter.
Nothing can compare anymore to us anymore.
You big good oak limb. I'm in such cute like w/ you today.

    In one diary of my have-beens, my mother
named me Elizabeth after one of her
mothers. You god particle. You matrilineage.
           I've never lived anywhere more
or less this haunted. She named my sister
Elizabeth. You boy
      genius. You midsummer pinky promise ring.

There's this person I know I'm not in love w/ but wears
a dress patterned like a postcard from the state my grandma
        died in. Imagine waking up
a whole frame away from your bedsheets. Imagine
      waking up & being anything as yellow
as a dress. You treeline. You root song. What's an amount
                of time equal
to you? You kindling ring finger. You unchewable bark
but the headache's gone. Pardon me, dandelions,
      have you seen my ghost, six foot nothing,

has an interstate for a mother but also a mother? Adjust
      your spurs, honey bunch. This time I'm writing all of us
in pink ink. Let's huckle-buckle off into the leafiest
      of all possible genderings. You know how the rain
starts right after you get home & the country song
      your friend slow danced w/ her big love to, the one
your mom would play real quiet on her moonbeam
      highway streak back to Pensacola, is somehow
already at the chorus & you forget there are words like joy?
      Or when someone whispers *Imagine you never met them*
back at the bum, grinning stars? You remember.
                              It's like that.
Or, is that. The difference between salt & salt. A someday
                   of matching sweaters.
Told you it's cute. O sweaters. O little knit
      bundles of vegetable-spit. It's always sunsetting.

You golden hour. You soap-soft seasonal.
                  Once my mom found me
sitting in a circle of candles, touching each rosebud
      & sat with me until we were wax museums
         of our secrets. Look—
the sky's a toenail & the moon's a chesthair. All the shirtless
      boys have tired themself out, spreadeagled
& slapping the sun off their shoulder blades. My body is a line
      heading for my body. You crushed-grass
sex smell. You dirt inverted comma. Someone w/ bleached
      hair is biking home to restud their denim.
I rediscovered kissing foreheads & it is so yes again.

      The light's seltzer, bubbles.
          I said *My lord*. I thought
My god. O moonstruck. O gladracket. Barring
      gravity, our knees could be forevering each other.

Barring leather, love is a world I'm praying
            all my mothers' joy back towards.

Hurry up & sunspot, daylilies!
            The cops aren't going to awe themselves
      to death & we have
                  a dictionary to laugh across.

Elizabeth was my name. I'm writing this on all the trees like a wish.
      I'm kissing every hem in sight.

We're all hysterical & going nowhere together.

                  C'mon rapture. Let's go bedazzling.

Nothing gets futured without its own spitshine
& I'm already not not not not not not miraculous.

DREAM ENDING IN A HOST OF ANGELS ZIPPING ME INTO MY GRANDMOTHER'S DRESS

Once & could-be-future girl, believe we're not like you. Sure,
the pickup was tucked in dusk, shed all carefree w/ its sunburn
shimmer. Still nothing new to say about the creek, how reeds
get moony, or when we saw pelicans hold hands & gossip.
But y'all must wanna get this close to soft, so here goes: spool
heels, silver sleeves w/ pink accents, kind to stifle the trailer
static, same color Dot says Granny passed in. Past since good
& we did keep her pearls for you, kissed the hems holy, darned
the moth marks back to true. Goes: none of it imitation. Goes:
we are her barefoot bloodline, butter in the salt pan. Trust
you're not from this sweat but still a goodness. You once most
only boy in the yard, laugh into your born polish. Step-joy,
uncousin: home is a name you bless in silk & cinch. Believe
we're all alive here. Come hum this lace blood-warm. Glisten.

FROM RECONSTRUCTIONS

> *all the world began with a yes*
> —Clarice Lispector

South star an ocean pulls you towardly yes come closer.

What's heaven is a question of who wears whose furs and cop-blood on the overpass.

There's nothing grass about you we hear ourselves saying to an exit sign's disaster of green.

His tongue on your stubble like a punched-through drum.

Past the abandoned blackberry stand, past the Safeway parking lot your knees untune at the sound.

Someone on fire coming down the driveway as though they were on fire.

Past the station wagon your aunt left on the side of the road, some pelicans punctuating what was its color.

A honey-fat bee quizzing the window frame.

Other worlds are possible, depending on how long ago you were a boy.

For example if none of us died today.

There's a pronoun at the end of this and it is not I.

The window frame, perhaps, the color of someone's nipples.

Past the smell of rosewater, lemongrass, crushed pine.

From here you can almost see the statues unfucked from their skylines, flags going up in smoke.

Heaven's a road trip, sweetheart, catch up.

This question of whose blood on your hand for a highway like that.

For a mouth like that.

How else can we describe it.

And the fire ants, and the gnat-clouds, and the street lamp was one kind of alive.

Minus even one word a sentence becomes outside of itself.

Biking home and the rain your face flowers.

Some cops spangling the air like cops.

What if because you strung fairy lights around your bathroom mirror.

Past where in another life you would have let his ryegrass ruin the back of your dress.

A pronoun occupying the air so nationally.

What if the opposite of grammatical is ring-bearer.

The aesthetics of cum are also its politics.

For example if only a fascist died today.

Past the part of the past your dress wasn't left to dirty near, the deadnettle freckling its once.

Imagine for example a chandelier a rust of comet-light.

And the laundry detergent, and the turned over yard chair, and the stadium across from the catfish spot.

Where a deerstand bows back into the grass, a doe nuzzling the old wood.

In a letter you wrote, you said rosing instead of rising.

As in, the water rosing to meet you.

Our sky harboring a fugitive twilight.

And the sunflower seeds catching gold on the dashboard like lace.

Any evidence of touch begins with a chorus line moving like firelight on badge-brass.

A cop trapped in a nightclub is still a cop and trapped in a nightclub.

There's nothing boyfriend about you, we heard you trying to unsay to the fig trees.

And the basketball court, and the ryegrass, and the way your aunt taught you to say Mississippi.

What if the opposite of bug-zapper is your grandmother's hand on the lid of her seed jar.

And your back in the fescue and his neck in the starlight.

Remembering anything is so science fiction of us.

Somewhere it is probably always New Orleans and somewhere else it is even more probably summer.

Some goldenrod spitting its girlhood, its copless locks & dam-water.

For example if we laughed today.

Time done the other way is still time.

Your mother pressing her palm to the bluegrass to the eyebright and arrowheads.

We walked to the property line and marked with speaking everywhere that history touched us.

A slow dance, a harness.

Your cousin's headstone announcing her smile and the fescue.

And the mockingbird staining the air with her minutes.

That it touches us everywhere.

Past where the road gives way to the water & the water gives way to its August.

Our backs arched to warm the shore with yes.

Even closer.

And cigarettes, and cinder blocks, and gun oil, and all over your blouse.

We labor at twilight and daybreak and rust.

We free the rain to its astonishment of falling.

Our headlamps, our cops, our exit signs.

What if none of us began with names.

Imagine that.

Time enough.

And world.

What is possible is not what is possible to say.

But we have been here before.

Two moons spackling the sky; brakelights in your mouth.

You good thing.

You lucky rucksack of doors.

Again.

South star and the ocean at our backs.

At our backs.

Makes us a paradise.

Paradise at our backs makes us a paradise.

And the branches of the linden rosing to touch the branches.

Yes.

It's supposed to be this bright.

The world is the closed door. It is a barrier.
And at the same time it is the way through.

—Simone Weil

TINNITUS

Everyone choirs and I like the light of her. Honey on the doorjamb.
Muscleheart moon. Listen. We'll make the night handstand for us.
And already. Castle in the sky like a hot stove coil. Say the heart was

a door we licked into metal. Say we left our rings on. She's percussion
on top of me like I'm what comes after we catch a bouquet. So what.
From some directions we're mostly water. And she's looking already.

On his knees. Like that. On my knees. And already. Everyone in her dark
floral nightgown. Me in my drumline of lipstick. Hands or ears, Dad says.
Sky strung like a jackknife. Young man he'd say. You can only pick one.

And the moon on his knees. And my glasses on the nightstand. Says
she'll wick away the metal. Choirs again. It's like light, y'know?
The king makes the music and the queen. And the queen. I'm looking

like a bone through the water at us. Almost touching. And the band
opening their bouquets like doors. Everyone's dizzy with flowers
and yes. Young man he'd say. Glass boy he'd choir. You know?

She already sounds like honey from here. Like water from here. Draws
the lipstick on so the rings sing along. And the queen. When I was
everyone the underwire just felt like hands. I liked that. And again.

The king was in the castle and the sky was in the mirror. On his knees.
He's laughing and the garden. On my hands. So what. I took a moon
in my mouth to prove I could. The sky sounding like tripwire. Everyone

in the doorlight. You know? When I was the king I chose hands. Listen.
Dad's in the kitchen and his hand on the hemline. And his hand
on a knife. Young man. In my mouth and you like that. The king was

in the sky and the garden. And the garden. Almost touching him.
Like metal from here. Everyone and the water on the nightstand.
Sky like a mirror so we all sing along. I'm cymbal and crashing.

She's kickdrum and yes. Yes. Strung like bouquets in the bonelight.
Floral nightgowns. Dark lipstick. Ring on each dizzy thumb. Listen.
Like that. From anywhere we are almost like each other. The moon

is a choir and the sky is a song. We've been here before. So what.
We all sang along and she likes that. She's laughing. Say the king
was in the sky and now he's music. And the queen like the doorlight

around us. Let me show you, you'd say. Ricket and hemline.
Ring finger and spit. My glasses on the nightstand. Listen. The sky
was glass until we made it a mirror. She's laughing and it's music

from here. She's music from here. How I'm almost like that.
And then I'm like that. Is it obvious yet? Everyone's hands
and the moonstruck air. My ears and every hemline sighing like yes.

All along we've been humming new homes for each other.
Like that. Let us show you, we'd say. The heart is a door
and we leave it open all night. Say yes. From everywhere else

we're mostly metal. Until we're music. Until the stars came.
The stars came. They took us back.

ACKNOWLEDGMENTS

The inscription is salvaged from Jaleh Mansoor's book *Marshall Plan Modernism: Italian Postwar Abstraction and the Beginnings of Autonomia* (Duke University Press, 2016) and Gillian Welch's song "I Dream A Highway."

The Simone Weil epigraph is from *Gravity & Grace* (Routledge, 2002).

Abiding thanks to the editors and staffs of the journals and magazines that many of these poems appeared in: *The Adroit Journal*, *The Arkansas International*, *BOAAT*, *The Cortland Review*, *jubilat*, *Poetry*, *Redivider*, *The Shallow Ends*, and *Washington Square Review*.

The poem "Hearing Loss" takes the line "a bad bad bad girl" from the poet Ewan Hill.

Sections of "from *Reconstructions*," often in previous forms, were published in *Diagram*, *Poetry*, *Tinderbox Poetry Journal*, and *Witness*, as well as in *Nat. Brut* as part of the folio 'Reclamation and Restoration: Redefining the Conversation about the South,' edited by Diamond Forde. That poem doesn't end here, but I'm grateful to those journals and editors for being a home to its pieces. The epigraph for "from *Reconstructions* (South star an ocean)" is from Clarice Lispector's *The Hour of the Star*, translated by Benjamin Moser (New Directions, 2011).

Everything I write was, is, and will be dedicated to librarians.

Thanks, too, to all the folks who have encouraged, edited, or given me space to write and think: Peter LaBerge, Peter Shippy, Anna Ross, Nicole Terez Dutton, Sophie Klahr, Richard Hoffmann, Tiana Clark, Katerina Gonzalez Seligmann, John Trimbur, and Maria Koundoura.

To Bryan Borland & Seth Pennington: Sibling Rivalry was the only home I ever wanted for this book.

I'm profoundly grateful to all my relations, blood and otherwise. I'm especially grateful to these people for their enduring friendships & impact on these poems: Yujane Chen, Myles Taylor, Brandon Melendez, George Abraham, Ewan Hill, Jess Rizkallah, Lyrik Courtney, Chase Berggrun, Zenaida Peterson,

Canese Jarboe, Nabila Lovelace, Billy Rebholz, Michelle Betters, Golden, and everyone at FEMS. To C., who too much of this was for to not say.

To Noah Baldino, for holding me to what language can do. To Sara Mae, without whom this version of the book would not exist.

To Kaveh Akbar, my teacher, my friend—my debt to you is everywhere.

To Grayson & Ellie. To my parents.

To everyone who ever thought another world was possible & stepped toward it: "Il y a un autre monde mais il est dans celui-ci" (Éluard).

Above all, to my grandmothers, Unkie & Virginia: it is just with you I follow.

ABOUT THE POET

Bradley Trumpfheller is from Alabama & Virginia. Their work has appeared in *Poetry*, *The Nation*, *jubilat*, *Indiana Review*, and elsewhere. They co-edit *Divedapper* & currently live in Massachusetts.

ABOUT THE PRESS

Sibling Rivalry Press is an independent press based in Little Rock, Arkansas. It is a sponsored project of Fractured Atlas, a nonprofit arts service organization. Contributions to support the operations of Sibling Rivalry Press are tax-deductible to the extent permitted by law, and your donations will directly assist in the publication of work that disturbs and enraptures. To contribute to the publication of more books like this one, please visit our website and click *donate*.

Sibling Rivalry Press gratefully acknowledges the following donors, without whom this book would not be possible:

Anonymous (18)
Arkansas Arts Council
John Bateman
W. Stephen Breedlove
Dustin Brookshire
Sarah Browning
Billy Butler
Asher Carter
Don Cellini
Nicole Connolly
Jim Cory
Risa Denenberg
John Gaudin
In Memory of Karen Hayes
Gustavo Hernandez
Amy Holman
Jessica Jacobs & Nickole Brown
Paige James
Nahal Suzanne Jamir
Allison Joseph
Collin Kelley
Trevor Ketner

Andrea Lawlor
Anthony Lioi
Ed Madden & Bert Easter
Mitchell, Blackstock, Ivers & Sneddon, PLLC
Stephen Mitchell
National Endowment for the Arts
Stacy Pendergrast
Simon Randall
Paul Romero
Randi M. Romo
Carol Rosenfeld
Joseph Ross
In Memory of Bill Rous
Matthew Siegel
Alana Smoot
Katherine Sullivan
Tony Taylor
Leslie Taylor
Hugh Tipping
Guy Traiber
Mark Ward
Robert Wright

9 781943 977727